PRENTICE HALL

Motion, Forces, and Energy

Guided Reading and Study Workbook

Student Edition

Prentice Hall

Needham, Massachusetts
Upper Saddle River, New Jersey
Glenview, Illinois

ISBN 0-13-054252-0

5 6 7 8 9 10   05 04 03 02

Motion, Forces, and Energy

© Prentice-Hall, Inc.

CHAPTER 1

MOTION

SECTION 1-1 **Describing and Measuring Motion** (pages 16-25)

This section explains how to recognize when an object is in motion and how to determine how fast it is moving.

▶ Recognizing Motion (pages 17–18)

1. An object is in _____ when its distance from another object is changing.

2. What is a reference point? _____

   _____

3. An object is in motion if it changes position relative to a(n) _____

   _____.

▶ Describing Distance (pages 18–19)

4. Complete the table about SI.

SI	
Question	**Answer**
What is its whole name?	
What number is it based on?	
What is its basic unit of length?	

5. How many centimeters are there in a meter? _____

6. How many meters are there in a kilometer? _____

CHAPTER 1, **Motion** *(continued)*

▶ **Calculating Speed** (pages 20–21)

7. What is the formula used to calculate the speed of an object?

   _____

8. How would you find the average speed of a cyclist throughout an entire

   race? _____

   _____

▶ **Describing Velocity** (pages 22–25)

9. Speed in a given direction is called _____.

10. An approaching storm is moving at 15 km/hr. What do you need to

    know to determine its velocity? _____

    _____

▶ **Graphing Motion** (pages 24–25)

11. The slant of a line on a graph is called its _____.

12. Is the following sentence true or false? The steepness of a motion
    graph's slope depends on how quickly or slowly the object is moving.

    _____

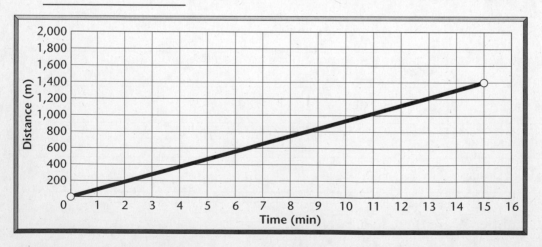

13. The motion graph above graphs the motion of a jogger on a run one

    day. How far did the jogger run in 15 minutes? _____

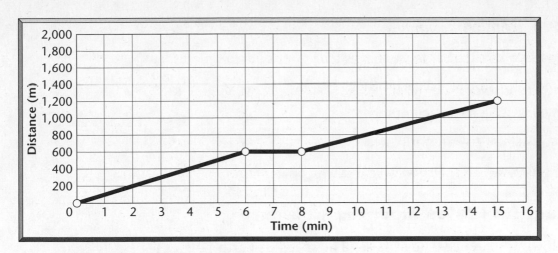

14. The motion graph above also shows the motion of a jogger on a run one day. The line is divided into segments. The middle segment is horizontal. What does that tell you about the jogger's progress between

minute 6 and minute 8? _____

_____

_____

· ·

**SECTION
1-2** **Slow Motion on Planet Earth**
(pages 28–31)

This section describes the movements of Earth's continents. It also gives a theory that explains why the continents move.

▶ What Are Earth's Plates? (pages 28–29)

1. Is the following sentence true or false? Earth's rocky outer shell is all one

   piece. _____

2. The upper layer of Earth consists of more than a dozen major pieces

   called _____.

3. What is the theory of plate tectonics? _____

   _____

   _____

CHAPTER 1, **Motion** *(continued)*

4. Circle the letter of each sentence that is true about Earth's plates.

   a. Some plates push toward each other.

   b. Some plates slide past each other.

   c. Earth consists of five major plates.

   d. Some plates pull away from each other.

▶ How Fast Do Plates Move? (pages 29–31)

5. Is the following sentence true or false? The speed of Earth's plates is very

   slow. _____

6. By knowing the average speed of a plate, what can scientists estimate

   about Earth's continents? _____

   _____

   _____

7. What formula do scientists use to predict how far a plate will move in a
   certain amount of time?

   _____

8. Is the following sentence true or false? The shapes and positions of

   Earth's continents will not change in the future. _____

9. A conversion factor is a fraction in which the numerator and the

   denominator are _____.

 Reading Skill Practice

By looking carefully at photographs and illustrations in textbooks, you can help yourself understand what you have read. Look carefully at Figure 8 on pages 30 and 31. What important idea does this illustration communicate? Do your work on a separate sheet of paper.

SECTION 1-3 Acceleration
(pages 34-38)

This section describes what happens to the motion of an object as it accelerates, or changes velocity. It also explains how to calculate acceleration.

▶ Acceleration in Science (pages 34–36)

1. What is acceleration? _____

_____

2. Acceleration involves a change in what two components?

_____

3. Any time the speed of an object increases, the object experiences

_____.

4. Is the following sentence true or false? Acceleration refers to increasing

speed, decreasing speed, or changing direction. _____

5. Deceleration is another word for negative _____.

6. Is the following sentence true or false? An object can be accelerating

even if its speed is constant. _____

7. Circle the letter of each sentence that describes an example of
acceleration.

a. A car follows a gentle curve in the road.

b. A batter swings a bat to hit a ball.

c. A truck parked on a hill doesn't move all day.

d. A runner slows down after finishing a race.

8. The moon revolves around Earth at a fairly constant speed. Is the moon

accelerating? _____

_____

CHAPTER 1, **Motion** *(continued)*

9. Use the table below to compare and contrast the meanings of *acceleration*.

Acceleration	
In Everyday Language	**In Scientific Language**
	Increasing speed
Slowing down	
Turning	

▶ Calculating Acceleration (pages 36–38)

10. What must you calculate to determine the acceleration of an object?

_____

_____

11. What is the formula you use to determine acceleration?

_____

12. Is the following sentence true or false? To calculate the acceleration of an automobile, you must first subtract the final speed from the initial

speed. _____

13. Circle the letter of each sentence that is true about calculating the acceleration of a moving object.

    a. If an object is moving without changing direction, then its acceleration is the change in its speed during one unit of time.

    b. If an object's speed changes by the same amount during each unit of time, then the acceleration of the object at any time is the same.

    c. To determine the acceleration of an object, you must calculate the change in velocity during only one unit of time.

    d. If an object's acceleration varies, then you can describe only average acceleration.

Motion, Forces, and Energy

14. Suppose velocity is measured in kilometers/hour and time is measured

in hours. What is the unit of acceleration? _____

▶ Graphing Acceleration (page 38)

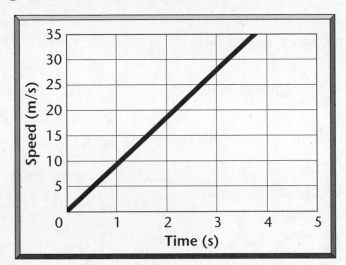

15. The graph above shows the motion of an object that is accelerating.

What happens to the speed of the object over time? _____

_____

_____

16. The graph line is slanted and straight. What does this line show about

the acceleration of the object? _____

_____

_____

17. Circle the letter of the sentence that is true when a graph of distance
versus time is a curved line.

a. The speed of the object never changes.

b. The distance traveled by the object varies each second.

c. The distance traveled by the object is the same each second.

d. The object does not accelerate.

CHAPTER 1, Motion (continued)

WordWise

Match each definition in the left column with the correct term in the right column. Then write the number of each term in the appropriate box below. When you have filled in all the boxes, add up the numbers in each column, row, and two diagonals. All the sums should be the same.

A. When an object's distance from another object is changing

B. A place or object used for comparison to determine if something is in motion

C. The system of measurement scientists use to communicate information clearly

D. The basic SI unit of length

E. The distance an object travels in one unit of time

F. Speed in a given direction

G. The total distance traveled divided by the total time

H. The major pieces of Earth's crust

I. The rate at which velocity changes

1. reference point
2. average speed
3. velocity
4. acceleration
5. speed
6. motion
7. meter
8. International System of Units (SI)
9. plates

= _____

A _____	B _____	C _____	= _____
D _____	E _____	F _____	= _____
G _____	H _____	I _____	= _____
= _____	= _____	= _____	= _____

Motion, Forces, and Energy

Name _____ Date _____ Class _____

MathWise

For the problems below, show your calculations. If you need more space, use another sheet of paper. Write the answers for the problems on the lines below.

▶ Calculating Speed (pages 20–21)

1. Speed = $\dfrac{32 \text{ m}}{8 \text{ s}}$ = _____

2. A car travels 66 kilometers in 3 hours. What is its speed?

Answer: _____

▶ Average Speed (page 21)

3. Average Speed = $\dfrac{200 \text{ km}}{5 \text{ hr}}$ = _____

4. Suppose a car travels 60 kilometers the first two hours and 15 kilometers the next hour. What is the car's average speed?

Answer: _____

5. Suppose you ride your bicycle into the countryside on a bike path. You travel 6 kilometers the first hour, 3 kilometers the second hour, and 6 kilometers the third hour. What is your average speed for the whole ride?

Answer: _____

CHAPTER 1, Motion (continued)

▶ Calculating Distance (pages 29–30)

6. Distance $= \dfrac{7\ cm}{1\ yr} \times 1{,}000\ yr = $ _____

7. Suppose one of Earth's plates moved 4 cm over the course of a year. How far will it move in 500 years?

   Answer: _____

▶ Calculating Acceleration (pages 36–38)

8. Acceleration $= \dfrac{20\ m/s - 4\ m/s}{4\ s} = $ _____

9. A cheetah accelerates from 2 m/s to 16 m/s in 7 seconds. What is the cheetah's average acceleration?

   Answer: _____

10. A motorcycle accelerates from rest to 31 m/s in 10 seconds. Find the motorcycle's average acceleration.

    Answer: _____

CHAPTER 2

FORCES

....

SECTION 2-1   The Nature of Force
(pages 44-49)

This section explains how balanced and unbalanced forces are related to motion. It also explains Newton's first law of motion.

▶ What Is Force? (pages 44–45)

1. In science, a force is _____.

2. When one object pushes or pulls another object, the first object is

   _____ a force on the second object.

3. Circle the letters of the two ways that forces are described.

   a. direction   **b.** velocity   **c.** strength   **d.** acceleration

▶ Unbalanced Forces (pages 45–46)

4. When two forces act in the same direction, they _____ together.

5. Adding a force acting in one direction to a force acting in another

   direction is the same as adding a(n) _____ number and

   a(n) _____ number.

6. Look at Figure 1 on page 45. What does the width of the arrows tell you

   about the forces they represent? _____

   _____

7. The overall force on an object after all the forces are added together is

   called the _____.

CHAPTER 2, Forces (continued)

8. The illustrations to the right represent ways that two forces can combine. Draw lines from the left column to the right column to show the result of each combination.

9. Unbalanced forces can cause an object to do three things. What are they?

_____

_____

10. Is the following sentence true or false? Unbalanced forces acting on an

object will change the object's motion. _____

11. Circle the letter of each sentence that is true about unbalanced forces.

a. When two forces act in opposite directions, the net force is the difference between the two forces.

b. When two forces act in the same direction, the net force is the difference between the two forces.

c. When two forces act in opposite directions, the net force is equal to the greater force.

d. When two forces act in the same direction, the net force is the sum of the two individual forces.

▶ Balanced Forces (pages 46–47)

12. Equal forces acting on one object in opposite directions are called

_____ .

13. Is the following sentence true or false? Balanced forces acting on an object will change the object's motion. _____

14. When you add equal forces exerted in opposite directions, the net force is _____.

▶ Newton's First Law of Motion (pages 48–49)

15. For an object to start moving, a(n) _____ has to act on it.

16. Is the following sentence true or false? Once an object is in its natural resting place, it cannot move by itself. _____

17. What is inertia? _____

_____

_____

18. What is Newton's first law of motion? _____

_____

_____

_____

19. Newton's first law of motion is also called the law of _____.

20. What explains why you continue moving forward if you are in a car that suddenly stops? _____

21. What is mass? _____

_____

22. What is the SI unit of mass? _____

23. The amount of inertia an object has depends on its _____.

24. How can mass be defined in terms of inertia? _____

_____

_____

CHAPTER 2, Forces *(continued)*

. . . .

SECTION 2-2 Force, Mass, and Acceleration
(pages 52-54)

This section explains how force and mass are related to acceleration.

▶ Newton's Second Law of Motion (pages 52–53)

1. What is Newton's second law of motion? _____

_____

_____

_____

2. What is the equation that describes the relationship among quantities of force, mass, and acceleration?

_____

3. Circle the letters of the two answers below that are different names for the same unit of measure.

a. m/s^2 **b.** N   **c.** kg • m/s^2 **d.** 1 kg

4. What equation for Newton's second law can you use to find acceleration?

_____

▶ Changes in Force and Mass (page 54)

5. How does an increase of force affect acceleration? _____

_____

_____

6. What are two ways you can increase the acceleration of an object?

_____

_____

7. How does an increase of mass affect acceleration? _____

_____

8. Is the following sentence true or false? One way to increase the force used to pull a wagon is to decrease the mass in the wagon.

_____

· ·

SECTION 2-3 **Friction and Gravity**
(pages 55-61)

This section describes the effects of friction on surfaces that rub on each other. It also describes how gravity acts between objects in the universe.

▶ Friction (pages 56–57)

1. Is the following sentence true or false? When two surfaces rub, the irregularities of one surface get caught on those of the other surface.

_____

2. What is friction? _____

_____

_____

3. Friction acts in a direction _____ to the object's direction of motion.

4. The strength of the force of friction depends on what two factors?

_____

_____

5. How is friction useful in helping you walk? _____

_____

_____

_____

CHAPTER 2, Forces *(continued)*

6. How does friction help an automobile move? _____

_____

_____

7. Complete the following table about the different kinds of friction.

Kinds of Friction	
Kind of Friction	**Friction Occurs When . . .**
	An object moves through a liquid or a gas
	Solid surfaces slide over each other
	An object rolls over a surface

8. Which kind of friction requires more force to overcome, rolling friction

or sliding friction? _____

9. What kind of friction occurs when moving parts have ball bearings?

_____

10. How does oil between machine parts reduce friction? _____

_____

_____

▶ Gravity (pages 58–60)

11. The force that pulls objects toward each other is called _____.

12. When is an object said to be in free fall? _____

_____

13. Near the surface of Earth, what is the acceleration of an object due to

the force of gravity? _____

14. An object that is thrown is called a(n) _____.

15. Is the following sentence true or false? An object that is dropped will hit the ground before an object that is thrown horizontally. _____

16. Objects falling through air experience a type of fluid friction called

_____.

17. Is the following sentence true or false? The greater the surface area of an object, the greater the air resistance. _____

18. On the diagram below, draw arrows that show the forces acting on the falling acorn. Label each arrow with the name of the force.

19. The greatest velocity a falling object reaches is called _____

_____.

20. What is weight? _____

_____

_____

21. How is weight different than mass? _____

_____

_____

22. Weight is usually measured in _____.

CHAPTER 2, Forces *(continued)*

▶ Universal Gravitation (pages 60–61)

23. Is the following sentence true or false? The force that makes an apple fall to the ground is the same force that keeps Earth orbiting the sun.

_____

24. What does the universal law of gravitation state? _____

_____

_____

25. Is the following sentence true or false? On the moon, your mass would be less than it is on Earth, but your weight would be the same.

_____

26. The force of attraction between two objects varies with what two

factors? _____

_____

SECTION 2-4 Action and Reaction (pages 64-69)

This section explains Newton's third law of motion. It also explains a law about moving objects.

▶ Newton's Third Law of Motion (pages 64–66)

1. What is Newton's third law of motion? _____

_____

_____

_____

2. What did Newton call the force exerted by the first object on a second

object? _____

© Prentice-Hall, Inc.

3. What did Newton call the force exerted by the second object back on

the first object? _____

4. The action and reaction forces in any situation will always be

_____ and _____.

5. Complete the flowchart below, which describes how a squid moves
through water.

Newton's Squid

A squid expels water out its back end. This is the

_____ force.

↓

The water expelled out of the back end of the squid pushes

back, exerting an equal and _____ force

on the squid. This is the _____ force.

↓

The squid moves _____ through the
water as a result of the reaction force.

6. Explain why the equal action and reaction forces do not cancel each

other when one person hits a ball. _____

_____

_____

_____

_____

CHAPTER 2, Forces *(continued)*

▶ Momentum (page 67)

7. The product of an object's mass and velocity is its _____.

8. What is the equation you use to determine the momentum of an object?

   _____

9. What is the unit of measurement for momentum? _____

   _____

▶ Conservation of Momentum (pages 68–69)

10. What does the law of conservation of momentum state? _____

    _____

    _____

11. Suppose a train car moving down a track at 10 m/s hits another train car that is not moving. Explain how momentum is conserved after the collision. _____

    _____

    _____

    _____

 ## Reading Skill Practice

A flowchart can help you remember the order in which a series of events occurs. Create a flowchart that describes how momentum is conserved when a moving train car collides with another moving train car. See your textbook on page 68. The first step in the flowchart will be this: One train car moves down a track at 10 m/s. The last step in the flowchart will be this: Momentum is conserved. Do your work on a separate sheet of paper. For more information about flowcharts, see page 211 in the Skills Handbook of your textbook.

SECTION 2-5 Orbiting Satellites
(pages 70-72)

This section explains how a rocket lifts off the ground and what keeps an object in orbit.

▶ How Do Rockets Lift Off? (pages 70–71)

1. Which of Newton's laws explains the lifting of a rocket into space?

   _____

2. When a rocket rises, what causes the action force? _____

   _____

   _____

3. When a rocket rises, what causes the reaction force? _____

   _____

   _____

4. On the diagram of a rocket lifting off the ground, draw and label arrows
   that show the action force and the reaction force.

CHAPTER 2, Forces *(continued)*

5. When a rocket lifts off the ground, the net force is in an upward direction. Is the upward pushing force greater or lesser than the downward pull of gravity? _____

▶ What Is a Satellite? (pages 71–72)

6. Any object that travels around another object in space is a(n)

   _____.

7. An object traveling in a circle is accelerating because it is constantly

   changing _____.

8. What is a force called that causes an object to move in a circle?

   _____

9. For a satellite, what is the centripetal force that causes it to move in a

   circle? _____

10. Is the following sentence true or false? Satellites in orbit around Earth

    continually fall toward Earth. _____

11. Explain why a satellite in orbit around Earth does not fall into Earth.

    _____

    _____

    _____

12. A satellite is a projectile that falls _____ Earth rather
    than into Earth.

13. Why doesn't a satellite need fuel to keep orbiting? _____

    _____

    _____

14. What force continually changes a satellite's direction? _____

WordWise

Use the clues to help you find the key terms from Chapter 2 hidden in the puzzle below. The terms may occur vertically, horizontally, or diagonally.

1. A _____ is a push or pull.

2. The overall force on an object after all forces are added together is called the _____ force.

3. The tendency of an object to resist change in its motion is called _____.

4. The amount of matter in an object is called _____.

5. One _____ equals the force required to accelerate 1 kilogram of mass at 1 meter per second per second.

6. The force that one surface exerts on another when the two rub against each other is called _____.

7. When solid surfaces slide over each other, the kind of friction that occurs is _____ friction.

8. The friction that occurs when an object moves through a fluid is called _____ friction.

9. The force that pulls objects toward Earth is _____.

10. When the only force acting on a falling object is gravity, the object is said to be in _____ fall.

11. Objects falling through air experience a type of fluid friction called _____ resistance.

12. The force of gravity on a person or object at the surface of a planet is known as _____.

13. The _____ of an object is the product of its mass and velocity.

14. Any object that travels around another object in space is a(n) _____.

```
m  q  m  o  m  e  n  t  u  m
a  f  g  i  n  e  r  t  i  a
s  o  r  l  i  o  l  n  g  f
s  r  a  i  q  a  z  y  n  r
w  c  v  p  c  f  r  e  e  i
w  e  i  g  h  t  a  e  w  c
u  p  t  f  l  u  i  d  t  t
i  e  y  c  n  i  r  o  o  i
n  s  l  i  d  i  n  g  n  o
s  a  t  e  l  l  i  t  e  n
```

CHAPTER 2, Forces *(continued)*

MathWise

For the problems below, show your calculations. If you need more space, use another sheet of paper. Write the answers for the problems on the lines below.

▶ Newton's Second Law of Motion (pages 52–53)

1. Force = 65 kg × 3m/s^2 = _____

2. A 250-kg trailer is being pulled by a truck. The force causes the trailer to accelerate at 4 m/s^2. What is the net force that causes this acceleration?

    Answer: _____

▶ Weight (pages 59–60)

3. Weight = 45 kg × 9.8 m/s^2 = _____

4. What is the weight of a rock that has a mass of 7 kg?

    Answer: _____

▶ Momentum (page 67)

5. Momentum = 5 kg × 6.5 m/s = _____

6. A baseball travels at 7 m/s, while a basketball moves at 3 m/s. The mass of the baseball is 0.14 kg and the mass of the basketball is 0.5 kg. Which

    has the greater momentum? _____

    _____

    _____

CHAPTER 3

FORCES IN FLUIDS

....

SECTION 3-1 **Pressure** (pages 78-83)

This section explains what causes pressure in fluids. It also describes how pressure changes with altitude and depth.

▶ **What Is Pressure?** (pages 78–80)

1. What do snowshoes do that makes it easier for the person wearing them to travel in deep snow? _____

   _____

   _____

2. Is the following sentence true or false? Force and pressure are the same thing. _____

3. What is pressure equal to? _____

   _____

   _____

4. Circle the letter of the term that is an SI unit of pressure.
   a. newton   **b.** liter   **c.** weight   **d.** pascal

5. Circle the letter of the *two* answers below that are equal to each other.
   a. 1 Pa   **b.** 1 N/cm^2 **c.** 1 N/m^2 **d.** 1 N

6. What unit of measure is used when a smaller unit is more practical for an area? _____

© Prentice-Hall, Inc.

CHAPTER 3, Forces in Fluids *(continued)*

7. Is the following sentence true or false? You can produce a lower

   pressure by decreasing the area a force acts on. _____

▶ Fluid Pressure (page 80)

8. A substance that can easily flow is a(n) _____.

9. Circle the letter of each of the following that are fluids.

   a. helium gas   **b.** liquid water   **c.** ice   **d.** air

10. Describe how molecules move in fluids. _____

    _____

    _____

    _____

11. What causes the pressure exerted by a fluid? _____

    _____

    _____

    _____

12. The pressure exerted by a fluid is the total force exerted by the fluid

    divided by the _____ over which the force is exerted.

▶ Fluid Pressure All Around (page 81)

13. What is another term for air pressure? _____

14. What causes air pressure? _____

    _____

▶ Balanced Pressures (pages 81–82)

15. Is the following sentence true or false? In a fluid that is not moving,
    pressure at a given point is exerted equally in all directions.

    _____

Motion, Forces, and Energy

16. On the illustration of the hand, draw arrows that indicate where the atmosphere is exerting air pressure on the hand. The size of each arrow should indicate the amount of air pressure on that part of the hand.

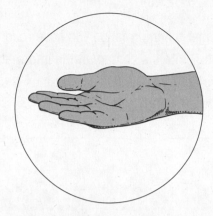

▶ Variations in Fluid Pressure (pages 82–83)

17. Is the following sentence true or false? Air pressure increases as elevation increases. _____

18. Why is air pressure lower at a higher elevation than at a lower elevation?

_____

_____

_____

_____

19. Is the following sentence true or false? Water pressure increases as depth increases. _____

20. Why is water pressure greater at a greater depth than at a shallow depth?

_____

_____

_____

21. The total pressure at a given point beneath the water results from the weight of the water above plus the weight of the _____ above it.

CHAPTER 3, Forces in Fluids *(continued)*

 Reading Skill Practice

Writing a summary can help you remember the information you have read. When you write a summary, write only the important points. Write a summary of the information under the heading *Fluid Pressure*, page 80. Your summary should be shorter than the text on which it is based. Do your work on a separate sheet of paper.

· ·

SECTION 3-2 **Transmitting Pressure in a Fluid**
(pages 86-89)

This section explains what Pascal's principle says about an increase in fluid pressure and describes how a hydraulic device works.

▶ **Pascal's Principle** (page 87)

1. What happens to the pressure in a bottle of water if you press the

   stopper at the top down farther? _____

   _____

   _____

2. What is the relationship known as Pascal's principle? _____

   _____

   _____

   _____

▶ **Force Pumps** (page 87)

3. What does a force pump do? _____

   _____

   _____

4. Describe the heart in terms of force pumps. _____

_____

_____

▶ Using Pascal's Principle (pages 88–89)

5. Suppose you push down on a small piston that is connected to a confined fluid, and another piston with the same area is connected by a U-shaped tube to the confined fluid. How much force will the second

piston experience compared to the first? _____

_____

_____

6. Suppose you push down on a small piston that is connected to a confined fluid, and a piston twenty times larger is connected by a U-shaped tube to the confined fluid. How much force will the larger

piston experience compared to the small piston? _____

_____

7. In a hydraulic system, how is the force applied on a small surface area

multiplied? _____

_____

_____

8. Is the following sentence true or false? A car's brake system multiples

the force of the driver's tap on the brake pedal. _____

9. The tube feet of a sea star take advantage of what principle to move

around? _____

10. When a sea star contracts different muscles, it changes the

_____ in the fluid of its tube foot.

11. The _____ a sea star exerts on the fluid in its system causes the tube foot to either push down or pull up on its sucker.

CHAPTER 3, Forces in Fluids (continued)

SECTION 3-3 **Floating and Sinking** (pages 90-96)

This section describes a force that acts on objects under water. It also explains why some objects float and others sink.

▶ Buoyancy (page 91)

1. Water exerts a(n) _____ force that acts on a submerged object.

2. Circle the letter of each sentence that is true about a buoyant force.

   a. It acts against the force of gravity.   **b.** It acts in an upward direction.

   c. It makes an object feel heavier.   **d.** It makes an object feel lighter.

3. How much fluid does a submerged object displace? _____

   _____

   _____

4. What does the Archimedes' principle state? _____

   _____

   _____

▶ Floating and Sinking (page 94)

5. Is the following sentence true or false? If the weight of a submerged object is less than the buoyant force, the object will sink.

   _____

6. What happens when the weight of a submerged object is exactly equal to

   the buoyant force? _____

   _____

   _____

Density (pages 94–96)

7. The _____ of a substance, no matter what state or shape, is its mass per unit volume.

8. What formula do you use to find density? _____

9. What is the density of water? _____

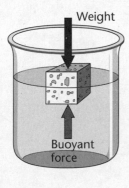 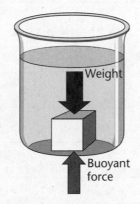 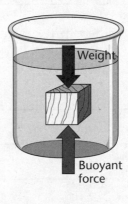

_____   _____   _____

10. The illustrations above show three objects in water. All three objects are equal in volume. The captions for these illustrations are listed below. Write the letter of the correct caption under each illustration.

    a. Object is more dense than water.

    b. Object is less dense than water.

    c. Object has a density that is equal to water's density.

11. Is the following sentence true or false? An object that is more dense than the fluid in which it is immersed floats to the surface.

    _____

12. An object that is _____ dense than the fluid in which it is immersed sinks.

13. Figure 16 on page 95 shows the densities of several substances. Use the figure to rank the following substances, from 1 for least dense to 3 for most dense.

    _____ **a.** corn syrup   _____ **b.** wood   _____ **c.** plastic

CHAPTER 3, Forces in Fluids *(continued)*

14. Why does a helium balloon rise in air while an ordinary balloon filled

with air does not? _____

_____

_____

15. When a submarine pumps water out of its flotation tanks, its density

decreases and it floats. Why does its density decrease? _____

_____

_____

16. Usually, the hull of a ship contains a large volume of air. Why?

_____

_____

17. The amount of fluid displaced by a submerged object depends on its

_____.

18. A ship stays afloat as long as the _____ force is greater
than its weight.

•••

SECTION 3-4 Applying Bernoulli's Principle
(pages 97-100)

This section explains how the pressure of a fluid is related to the motion of the fluid.

▶ Bernoulli's Principle (pages 97–98)

1. Is the following sentence true or false? The faster a fluid moves, the

more pressure the fluid exerts. _____

Motion, Forces, and Energy

2. What does Bernoulli's principle state? _____

_____

_____

3. Is the following sentence true or false? A faster-moving fluid exerts less

pressure than a slower-moving fluid. _____

4. Explain why a sheet of tissue paper rises when you blow air above the

tissue paper. _____

_____

_____

▶ Objects in Flight (pages 98–99)

5. Is the following sentence true or false? Objects can be designed so that
their shapes cause air to move at different speeds above and below them.

_____

6. If the air moves faster above an object, does pressure push the object

upward or downward? _____

7. If the air moves faster below an object, does pressure push the object

upward or downward? _____

8. On the illustration of a wing below, draw arrows that show the path of
air above and below the wing.

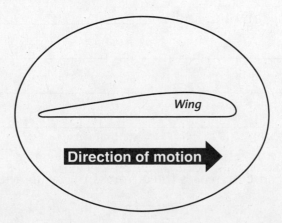

CHAPTER 3, Forces in Fluids *(continued)*

9. Air that moves over the top of an airplane wing must travel farther than air that moves along the bottom of the wing. As a result, the air moving over the top exerts less _____ than the air moving along the bottom.

10. What is lift? _____

_____

11. In what way is an airplane wing shaped like a bird's wing? _____

_____

12. Why is a spoiler on a racing car curved on the lower side? _____

_____

_____

_____

▶ Bernoulli's Principle at Home (pages 98–100)

13. How do differences in air pressure cause smoke to rise up a chimney?

_____

_____

_____

14. When you squeeze the rubber bulb of a perfume atomizer, how do you change the air pressure at the top of the tube? _____

_____

_____

_____

15. Is the following sentence true or false? An atomizer works because moving air at the top of the tube increases the air pressure inside the flask. _____

WordWise

Answer the questions by writing the correct key terms in the blanks. Use the circled letter in each term to find the hidden key term. Then write a definition for the hidden key term.

1. Whose principle states that when force is applied to a confined fluid, an increase in pressure is transmitted equally to all parts of the fluid?

   Ⓞ _ _ _ _ _

2. What is the force that acts in an upward direction, against the force of gravity, so it makes an object feel lighter?

   _ _ _ _ _ _ _   _ _ Ⓞ _ _

3. What kind of system multiplies by transmitting pressure to another part of a confined fluid?

   _ _ _ _ _ _ _ _ _ _   _ _ _ _ Ⓞ _

4. What is the unit of pressure equal to N/m^2?

   _ _ Ⓞ _ _ _

5. What is the measurement of how much mass of a substance is contained in a unit of volume?

   _ _ _ Ⓞ _ _ _

6. What is a substance that can easily flow?

   _ _ Ⓞ _ _

7. Whose principle states that the buoyant force on an object is equal to the weight of the fluid displaced by the object?

   _ Ⓞ _ _ _ _ _ _ _ _ _

8. Whose principle states that the pressure exerted by a moving stream of fluid is less than the pressure of the surrounding fluid?

   _ Ⓞ _ _ _ _ _ _ _ _

Key Term: _ _ _ _ _ _ _ _

Definition: _____

_____

CHAPTER 3, Forces in Fluids *(continued)*

MathWise

For the problems below, show your calculations. If you need more space, use another sheet of paper. Write the answers for the problems on the lines below.

▶ Calculating Pressure (pages 79–80)

1. Pressure $= \dfrac{20\ \text{N}}{10\ \text{m}^2} =$ _____

2. A force of 25 N is exerted on a surface with an area of 5 m². What is the pressure on that area?

   Answer: _____

3. A force of 160 N is exerted on a surface with an area of 40 m². What is the pressure on that area?

   Answer: _____

▶ Density (pages 94–95)

4. Density $= \dfrac{12\ \text{g}}{3\ \text{cm}^3} =$ _____

5. A substance has a mass of 30 g and a volume of 15 cm³. What is its density?

   Answer: _____

6. A substance has a volume of 20 cm³ and a mass of 10 g. What is its density?

   Answer: _____

CHAPTER 4

WORK AND MACHINES

SECTION 4-1 **What Is Work?** (pages 106-109)

This section explains the scientific meaning of work and describes how to calculate the work done on an object.

▶ **The Meaning of Work** (pages 106–108)

1. In scientific terms, when do you do work? _____

_____

_____

2. Complete the following table by classifying each example as either work or no work.

Work?	
Example	**Work or No Work?**
You pull your books out of your book bag.	
You lift a bin of newspapers.	
You push on a car stuck in the snow.	
You hold a heavy piece of wood in place.	
You pull a sled through the snow.	
You hold a bag of groceries.	

3. In order for you to do work on an object, the object must move some

_____ as a result of your force.

CHAPTER 4, Work and Machines *(continued)*

4. Explain why you don't do any work when you carry an object at a

   constant velocity. _____

   _____

   _____

   _____

5. When you pull a sled through the snow, why does only part of your

   force do work? _____

   _____

   _____

   _____

▶ Calculating Work (pages 108–109)

6. The amount of work you do depends on both the amount of

   _____ you exert and the _____ the object

   moves.

7. Is the following sentence true or false? Lifting a heavier object demands

   greater force than lifting a lighter object. _____

8. Is the following sentence true or false? Moving an object a shorter
   distance requires more work than moving an object a greater distance.

   _____

9. What formula do you use to determine the amount of work done on an

   object? _____

10. What is the SI unit of work? _____

11. What is the amount of work you do when you exert a force of 1 newton

    to move an object a distance of 1 meter? _____

SECTION 4-2 Mechanical Advantage and Efficiency
(pages 110-115)

This section explains how machines make work easier and describes how to calculate how efficient a machine is.

▶ What Is a Machine? (pages 110–112)

1. What is a machine? _____

_____

_____

2. Is the following sentence true or false? A machine decreases the amount

   of work needed to do a job. _____

3. Circle the letter of the sentences that are true about how a machine
   makes work easier.

   a. A machine makes work easier by multiplying force you exert.

   b. A machine makes work easier by reducing the amount of force needed
   to do the job.

   c. A machine makes work easier by multiplying the distance over which
   you exert force.

   d. A machine makes work easier by changing the direction in which you
   exert force.

4. The force you exert on a machine is called the _____.

5. The force exerted by the machine is called the _____.

6. Is the following sentence true or false? In some machines, the output

   force is greater than the input force. _____

7. If a machine allows you to use less force to do some amount of work, then

   you must apply the input force over a greater _____.

8. Is the following sentence true or false? In some machines, the output

   force is less than the input force. _____

CHAPTER 4, Work and Machines *(continued)*

9. Write labels on the illustration below to show which arrow represents the input force and which represents the output force.

▶ Mechanical Advantage *(page 113)*

10. What is a machine's mechanical advantage? _____

_____

_____

11. What is the formula you use to determine the mechanical advantage of a machine?

_____

12. In a machine that has a mechanical advantage of more than 1, the

_____ force is greater than the _____ force.

▶ Efficiency of Machines *(pages 114–115)*

13. In any machine, some work is wasted overcoming _____.

14. The comparison of a machine's output work to its input work is

_____.

15. What is the formula you use to calculate the efficiency of a machine?

_____

16. The mechanical advantage that a machine provides in a real situation is

called the _____ mechanical advantage.

17. The mechanical advantage of a machine without friction is called the

machine's _____ mechanical advantage.

Reading Skill Practice

By looking carefully at photographs and illustrations in textbooks, you can help yourself better understand what you have read. Look carefully at Figure 5 on page 111. What important idea does this illustration communicate?

SECTION 4-3 Simple Machines (pages 118-128)

This section describes the six kinds of simple machines. It also explains how to calculate the advantage of using simple machines.

▶ Introduction (page 118)

1. What are the six basic kinds of simple machines?

    a. _____   b. _____   c. _____

    d. _____   e. _____   f. _____

▶ Inclined Plane (pages 119–120)

2. What is an inclined plane? _____

    _____

3. What formula do you use to determine the ideal mechanical advantage of an inclined plane?

    _____

CHAPTER 4, Work and Machines *(continued)*

4. Circle the letter of each sentence that is true about inclined planes.

　　a. The necessary input force is less than the output force.

　　b. A ramp is an example of an inclined plane.

　　c. The necessary input force is more than the output force.

　　d. An inclined plane allows you to exert your force over a longer distance.

5. You can increase the _____ of an inclined plane by decreasing the friction.

▶ Wedge (page 120)

6. What is a wedge? _____

_____

_____

7. Is the following sentence true or false? In a wedge, the inclined plane itself moves. _____

8. Is the following sentence true or false? A wedge multiples force to do the job. _____

▶ Screws (page 121)

9. What is a screw? _____

_____

10. A spiral inclined plane forms the _____ of a screw.

11. When using a screwdriver to twist a screw into a piece of wood, where is the input force applied and where is the output force exerted?

_____

_____

_____

▶ Levers (pages 121–123)

12. What is a lever? _____

_____

_____

13. The fixed point that a lever pivots around is called the _____.

14. Circle the letter of each sentence that is true about levers.

   a. A lever increases the effect of your input force.

   b. There are three different types of levers.

   c. A lever changes the direction of your input force.

   d. The fulcrum is always located at the same place on a lever.

15. On each diagram below, draw a triangle below the lever to show where the fulcrum is located on each class of lever.

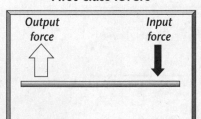
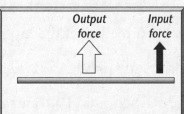
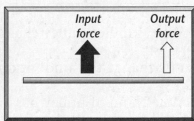

16. Complete the following table about levers.

Levers	
Class of Lever	**Examples**
	Door, wheel barrow, bottle opener
	Seesaw, scissors, pliers
	Baseball bat, shovel, rake

17. What formula do you use to calculate the ideal mechanical advantage of a lever?

_____

CHAPTER 4, Work and Machines *(continued)*

▶ Wheel and Axle (pages 124–126)

18. What is a wheel and axle? _____

_____

_____

19. What formula do you use to calculate the ideal mechanical advantage
of a wheel and axle?

_____

▶ Pulley (pages 126–127)

20. What is a pulley? _____

_____

_____

21. What kind of pulley changes the direction of the input force but does

not change the amount of force you apply? _____

22. What kind of pulley has an ideal mechanical advantage of 2?

_____

▶ Compound Machines (page 128)

23. What is a compound machine? _____

_____

24. What do you need to know to calculate the mechanical advantage of a

compound machine? _____

_____

_____

25. A system of _____ is a device with toothed wheels that
fit into one another.

© Prentice-Hall, Inc.

SECTION 4-4 Machines in the Human Body
(pages 132-134)

This section describes how the body uses natural levers and wedges.

▶ Living Levers (pages 132–134)

1. What do most of the levers in your body consist of? _____

_____

2. Your muscles are attached to your bones by tough connective tissue

called _____.

3. In a living lever in your body, what acts as the lever's fulcrum?

_____

_____

4. On the illustration of a living lever, label each arrow to show where the
   input force and the output force are located. Also show where the
   fulcrum is located.

▶ Working Wedges (page 134)

5. What simple machines do your incisors resemble? _____

6. Explain how your front teeth are like an ax. _____

_____

_____

_____

CHAPTER 4, Work and Machines *(continued)*

WordWise

Complete the sentences by using one of the scrambled words below.

Word Bank

lelyup   xela   oounmpdc   fiienycefc   ttuuop   veelr

euojl   deegw   tupni   rwko   wecrs   clruumf   iclndeni   enihcam

A device that is thick at one end and tapers to a thin edge at the other end is a(n)

_____.

A machine that utilizes two or more simple machines is called a(n) _____ machine.

The force exerted by a machine is called the _____ force.

The fixed point that a lever pivots around is called the _____.

You do _____ on an object when you exert a force on the object that causes the object to move some distance.

A wheel and _____ is a simple machine made of two circular or cylindrical objects that are fastened together and that rotate around a common axis.

The _____ of a machine compares the output work to the input work.

A rigid bar that is free to pivot, or rotate, about a fixed point is a(n) _____.

The force you exert on a machine is called the _____ force.

A(n) _____ plane is a flat, slanted surface.

A grooved wheel with a rope wrapped around it is a(n) _____.

A device with which you can do work in a way that is easier or more effective is a(n)

_____.

The SI unit of work is called the _____.

A(n) _____ can be thought of as an inclined plane wrapped around a cylinder.

Motion, Forces, and Energy

MathWise

For the problems below, show your calculations. If you need more space, use another sheet of paper. Write the answers for the problems on the lines below.

▶ Calculating Work (pages 108–109)

1. Work = 10 N × 35 m = _____

2. An elevator lifts a man with a weight of 500 N up three floors, or 30 m. How much work did the elevator do?

Answer: _____

▶ Mechanical Advantage (page 113)

3. Mechanical advantage = $\dfrac{60 \text{ N}}{15 \text{ N}}$ = _____

4. Suppose you exert of force of 2,800 N to lift a desk up onto a porch. But if you use a ramp, you need to exert a force of only 1,400 N to push it up the ramp onto the porch. What is the mechanical advantage of the ramp?

Answer: _____

▶ Calculating Efficiency (pages 114–115)

5. Efficiency = $\dfrac{100 \text{ J}}{200 \text{ J}}$ × 100% = _____

6. You do 4,000 J of work using a sledge hammer. The sledge hammer does 3,000 J of work on the spike. What is the efficiency of the sledge hammer?

Answer: _____

CHAPTER 4, Work and Machines *(continued)*

▶ Advantage of an Inclined Plane (page 119)

7. Ideal mechanical advantage $= \dfrac{8\ m}{2\ m} =$ _____

8. Suppose you built a ramp to the front door of the post office for people using wheel chairs. The post office door is 3 m above the level of the sidewalk. The ramp you build is 15 m long. What is the ideal mechanical advantage of your ramp?

Answer: _____

▶ Advantage of a Lever (page 122)

9. Ideal mechanical advantage $= \dfrac{4\ m}{2\ m} =$ _____

10. Suppose you held the handles of a wheel barrow 2.4 m from where they are attached to the wheel. The heavy stone in the wheel barrow was 1.2 m from the wheel. What is the ideal mechanical advantage of the wheel barrow?

Answer: _____

▶ Advantage of a Wheel and Axle (pages 125–126)

11. Ideal mechanical advantage $= \dfrac{36\ cm}{3\ cm} =$ _____

12. Suppose the radius of your bicycle's wheel is 30 cm. The radius of the bicycle's axle is just 5 cm. What is the ideal mechanical advantage of that wheel and axle?

Answer: _____

CHAPTER 5

ENERGY AND POWER

· ·

SECTION 5–1 The Nature of Energy
(pages 140-145)

This section explains how work and energy are related. It also identifies the two basic kinds of energy and describes some different forms of energy.

▶ **What Is Energy?** (pages 140–141)

1. The ability to do work or cause change is called _____.

2. Why can work be thought of as the transfer of energy? _____

_____

_____

▶ **Kinetic Energy** (pages 141–142)

3. What are the two general kinds of energy?

    a. _____   b. _____

4. What is kinetic energy? _____

5. The kinetic energy of an object depends on both its _____

    and its _____.

6. Kinetic energy increases as velocity _____.

7. What formula do you use to calculate kinetic energy?

_____

8. Because velocity is squared in the kinetic energy equation, doubling an

    object's velocity will _____ its kinetic energy.

CHAPTER 5, Energy and Power (continued)

▶ Potential Energy (pages 142–143)

9. What is potential energy? _____

_____

10. What is the potential energy called that is associated with objects that

can be stretched or compressed? _____

11. What is potential energy called that depends on height? _____

_____

12. What is the formula you use to determine the gravitational potential

energy of an object? _____

13. Is the following sentence true or false? The greater the height of an

object, the greater its gravitational potential energy. _____

▶ Different Forms of Energy (pages 144–145)

14. What is mechanical energy? _____

_____

15. What is thermal energy? _____

_____

_____

16. Is the following sentence true or false? When the thermal energy of an

object increases, its particles move faster. _____

17. The potential energy stored in chemical bonds that hold chemical

compounds together is called _____.

18. What kind of energy is stored in the foods you eat? _____

19. The energy that moving electric charges carry is called

_____ energy.

© Prentice-Hall, Inc.

▶ Conservation of Energy (pages 152–153)

7. What does the law of conservation of energy state? _____

_____

_____

8. Friction converts mechanical energy to _____ energy.

9. Circle the letter of the sentence that explains why no machine is 100 percent efficient.

   a. Electrical energy is converted to mechanical energy by fuel.

   b. Mechanical energy is converted to thermal energy by friction.

   c. Thermal energy is converted to mechanical energy by friction.

   d. Mechanical energy is converted to electrical energy by a spark.

10. How did Albert Einstein's theory of relativity change the law of

    conservation of energy? _____

_____

_____

_____

11. Is the following sentence true or false? Matter can sometimes be

    converted to energy. _____

▶ Conserving Energy (page 153)

12. Compare and contrast the meanings of *conserving energy* in the table.

	Conserving Energy
In Environmental Science	
In Physical Science	

CHAPTER 5, Energy and Power *(continued)*

· ·

SECTION 5-3 **Energy Conversions and Fossil Fuels**
(pages 154-157)

This section explains the source of the energy stored in fossil fuels and describes how energy is converted when fossil fuels are used.

▶ Formation of Fossil Fuels (pages 155–157)

1. Is the following sentence true or false? A fuel is a material that stores chemical potential energy. _____

2. Circle the letters of the following that are fossil fuels.
   a. coal   **b.** sunlight   **c.** petroleum   **d.** natural gas

3. Where did the energy in fossil fuels originally come from?
   _____

4. What energy conversion takes place on the sun? _____
   _____
   _____

5. What energy conversion takes place during photosynthesis?
   _____
   _____

▶ Use of Fossil Fuels (page 157)

6. How is the potential chemical energy of fossil fuels released?
   _____

7. The process of burning fossil fuels is known as _____.

8. What energy conversion occurs during combustion? _____
   _____
   _____

       Motion, Forces, and Energy

9. In a modern coal-fired power plant, the mechanical energy of turbines

is converted into electrical energy by _____.

....

SECTION 5-4 **Power** (pages 158–162)

This section describes how you calculate power and explains the difference between power and energy.

▶ What Is Power? (pages 158–159)

1. What is power? _____

_____

_____

2. Is the following sentence true or false? You exert more power when you run up a flight of stairs than when you walk up the stairs.

_____

3. Circle the letter of each sentence that is true about a device that is twice as powerful as another device.

   a. The more powerful device can do half the amount of work in half the time.

   b. The more powerful device can do the same amount of work in half the time.

   c. The more powerful device can do twice the amount of work in the same amount of time.

   d. The more powerful device can do twice the amount of work in twice the amount of time.

4. What is the formula you use to calculate power?

_____

5. Rewrite the equation for power in a way that shows what work equals.

_____

© Prentice-Hall, Inc.

CHAPTER 5, Energy and Power *(continued)*

6. 1 J/s = 1 _____

7. Is the following sentence true or false? Power is often measured in

larger units than watts. _____

8. 1 kilowatt = _____ watts

9. Is the following sentence true or false? An electric power plant produces

millions of kilowatts. _____

▶ Power and Energy (pages 160–161)

10. Is the following sentence true or false? Power is limited to situations in

which objects are moved. _____

11. Power is the _____ at which energy is transferred from
one object to another or converted from one form to another.

12. The power of a light bulb is the rate at which _____

energy is converted into _____ energy and

_____ energy.

13. Why is a 100-watt light bulb brighter than a 40-watt light bulb?

_____

_____

_____

▶ Horsepower (page 162)

14. Circle the letter of each sentence that is true about the unit known as
horsepower.

a. Horsepower is an SI unit of power.

b. James Watt used the word *horsepower* to compare the work of a
steam engine with the work of a horse.

c. People use the unit horsepower when talking about automobile engines.

d. 1 horsepower = 746 watts

WordWise

Complete the following paragraphs using the list of words and phrases below. Each word or phrase is used only once.

Word Bank

law of conservation of energy   nuclear energy   kinetic energy   thermal energy
fossil fuels   electromagnetic energy   energy conversion   electrical energy
power   energy   mechanical energy   potential energy   chemical energy

In nature, things are constantly changing, and the identification of what causes changes is important in physical science. The ability to do work or cause change is called _____. There are two general kinds of energy. The energy of motion is called _____. Energy that is stored and held in readiness is called _____.

There are different forms of the two general kinds of energy. The energy associated with the motion or position of an object is called _____. The total energy of the particles of an object is called _____. The potential energy stored in chemical bonds that hold chemical compounds together is called _____. The energy that moving electric charges carry is called _____. Visible light and ultraviolet rays are forms of _____. The energy stored in the nucleus of an atom is _____.

Most forms of energy can be converted into other forms. A change from one form of energy to another is called _____. Such changes from one form of energy to another do not mean any energy is lost. The _____ states that when one form of energy is converted to another, no energy is destroyed in the process.

A fuel is a material that stores chemical potential energy. For many purposes, we use _____, such as coal, petroleum, and natural gas. The energy conversions in modern coal-fired power plants result in the electricity you use for home electrical devices. You use these devices to do work. The rate at which work is done, or the amount of work done in a unit of time, is called _____.

CHAPTER 5, Energy and Power *(continued)*

MathWise

For the problems below, show your calculations. If you need more space, use another sheet of paper. Write the answers for the problems on the lines below.

▶ Calculating Gravitational Potential Energy (page 143)

1. Gravitational potential energy = 25 N × 10 m = _____

2. A student stands at the edge of a diving board that is 3 m high. The student's weight is 350 N. What is the student's gravitational potential energy?

   Answer: _____

3. Gravitational potential energy = 60 kg × 9.8 m/s^2 × 5 m = _____

4. Suppose a boulder has a mass of 25 kg, and it is perched on the edge of a cliff that is 45 m high. What is the gravitational potential energy of the boulder?

   Answer: _____

▶ Calculating Power (pages 158–159)

5. Power = $\dfrac{5{,}000 \text{ N} \times 15 \text{ m}}{3 \text{ s}}$ = _____

6. You exert a force of 300 N to lift a box 2 m from the floor to a shelf in 3 s. How much power did you use?

   Answer: _____

CHAPTER 6

THERMAL ENERGY AND HEAT

SECTION 6-1 Temperature and Thermal Energy
(pages 168-170)

This section describes the three common temperature scales and explains how temperature differs from thermal energy.

▶ **Temperature** (pages 168–169)

1. Is the following sentence true or false? All particles of matter have

   kinetic energy. _____

2. What is temperature? _____

   _____

   _____

3. Which particles are moving faster, the particles of a mug of hot cocoa or

   the particles of a glass of cold chocolate milk? _____

   _____

   _____

▶ **Temperature Scales** (pages 169–170)

4. What are the three common scales for measuring temperature?

   a. _____   b. _____   c. _____

5. The most common temperature scale in the United States is the

   _____ scale.

6. The temperature scale used in most of the world is the

   _____ scale.

CHAPTER 6, Thermal Energy and Heat *(continued)*

7. The temperature scale commonly used in physical science is the

   _____ scale.

8. What are the intervals on the Fahrenheit scale called?

   _____

9. Which scale is divided into 100 equal parts between the freezing and

   boiling points of water? _____

10. What is the temperature called at which no more energy can be

    removed from matter? _____

11. Complete the following table. See Figure 2 on page 169.

Temperature Scales			
Scale	Absolute zero	Water freezes	Water boils
Fahrenheit	−460°		
	−273°		100°
	0	273	

▶ Thermal Energy (page 170)

12. The total energy of the particles in a substance is called

    _____ energy.

13. Circle the letter of each sentence that is true of thermal energy.

    a. Thermal energy partly depends on the temperature of a substance.

    b. Thermal energy partly depends on the scale used to measure the
       temperature of a substance.

    c. Thermal energy partly depends on how the particles of a substance
       are arranged.

    d. Thermal energy partly depends on the number of particles of a
       substance.

SECTION 6-2 The Nature of Heat
(pages 171–177)

This section explains how heat is related to thermal energy and describes three ways heat is transferred.

▶ Introduction (pages 171–172)

1. What is heat? _____

_____

_____

_____

2. Is the following sentence true or false? Heat is thermal energy moving

from a warmer object to a cooler object. _____

▶ How Is Heat Transferred? (pages 172–174)

3. Circle the letter of the three ways that heat can move.

   a. conduction   **b.** current   **c.** radiation   **d.** convection

4. Think of a metal spoon in a pot of hot water. How do the particles of

the water affect the particles of the spoon? _____

_____

_____

_____

5. How is heat transferred in convection? _____

_____

_____

6. The circular motion of fluid caused by rising and sinking of heated and

cooler fluid is known as a(n) _____.

CHAPTER 6, Thermal Energy and Heat *(continued)*

7. The illustration shows a pot of liquid on a stovetop burner. Draw the convection currents that result.

8. Is the following sentence true or false? Radiation requires matter to

   transfer energy. _____

9. Complete the table.

Heat Transfer		
Process	**How Heat Moves**	**Example**
Conduction		
Convection		
Radiation		

▶ Heat Moves One Way (page 174)

10. When heat flows from one substance to another, what happens to the temperature of the substance giving off the heat and to the temperature

    of the substance receiving the heat? _____

    _____

    _____

    _____

11. Why can't ice transfer coldness into another substance? _____

_____

_____

▶ Conductors and Insulators (pages 175–176)

12. A material that conducts heat well is called a(n) _____.

13. A material that does not conduct heat well is called a(n)

_____.

14. Classify each of the following materials as either a conductor or an insulator by writing the correct term on the line.

a. air _____ **b.** wool _____

c. wood _____ **d.** tile _____

e. silver _____ **f.** fiberglass _____

▶ Specific Heat (pages 176–177)

15. What is a substance's specific heat? _____

_____

_____

16. What is the unit of measure for specific heat? _____

_____

17. Materials with a high specific heat can absorb a great deal of thermal

energy without a great change in _____.

18. The energy gained or lost by an object is related to which of the following? Circle the letter of the terms that answer the question.

a. mass **b.** volume **c.** specific heat **d.** temperature

19. What is the formula you can use to calculate thermal energy changes?

_____

CHAPTER 6, Thermal Energy and Heat *(continued)*

SECTION 6-3 **Thermal Energy and States of Matter**
(pages 181-186)

This section explains what causes matter to change state. It also explains why matter expands when it is heated.

▶ **Three States of Matter** (page 182)

1. Is the following sentence true or false? Most matter can exist in three states.

_____

2. Circle the letter of the terms that identify states of matter.

    a. water   **b.** gas   **c.** liquid   **d.** solid

3. The particles that make up a(n) _____ are packed together in a relatively fixed position.

4. Circle the letter of each statement that is true about liquids.

    a. Liquids have a definite volume.

    b. Liquids have a fixed shape.

    c. Liquid particles can move around.

    d. Liquid particles are moving around so fast that they don't even stay close together.

5. In which state of matter can the particles only vibrate back and forth?

_____

6. In which state of matter do the particles expand to fill all the space

available? _____

▶ **Changes of State** (pages 182–183)

7. What is a change of state? _____

_____

_____

8. Circle the letter of each sentence that is true.

   a. The particles of a gas move faster than the particles of a liquid.

   b. The particles of a solid move faster than the particles of a gas.

   c. The particles of a liquid move faster than the particles of a solid.

   d. The particles of a gas move faster than the particles of a solid.

9. Matter will change from one state to another if _____ is absorbed or released.

10. On the graph below, write labels for the regions of the graph that represent the gas, liquid, and solid states of matter.

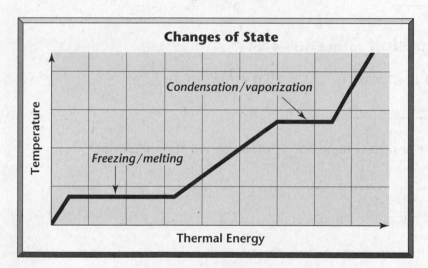

► Solid–Liquid Changes of State (pages 183–184)

11. The change in state from a solid to a liquid is called _____.

12. The temperature at which a solid changes to a liquid is called the

    _____.

13. The change in state from a liquid to a solid is called _____.

14. The temperature at which a substance changes from a liquid to a solid

    is called its _____.

► Liquid–Gas Changes of State (pages 184–185)

15. What is vaporization? _____

    _____

CHAPTER 6, Thermal Energy and Heat *(continued)*

16. If vaporization takes place on the surface of a liquid it is called

_____.

17. What is vaporization called when it occurs below the surface of a

liquid? _____

18. The temperature at which liquid boils is called its _____.

19. A change from the gas state to the liquid state is called

_____.

▶ Thermal Expansion (pages 185–186)

20. The expanding of matter when it is heated is known as

_____.

21. What happens to the liquid in a thermometer when it is heated?

_____

22. Heat-regulating devices are called _____.

23. In thermostats, what are strips of two different metals joined together

called? _____

24. In thermostats, bimetallic strips are used because different metals

_____ at different rates.

 # Reading Skill Practice

You can often increase your understanding of what you've read by making comparisons. A compare/contrast table helps you do this. On a separate sheet of paper, draw a table to compare the three states of matter as explained on page 182. The three row heads will be *Solid, Liquid,* and *Gas.* Column heads should include *State, Particles, Shape,* and *Volume.* For more information about compare/contrast tables, see page 210 in the Skills Handbook of your textbook.

● ●

SECTION 6-4 Uses of Heat (pages 187-190)

This section describes how thermal energy is related to heat engines and refrigerators.

▶ Heat Engines (pages 187–189)

1. To fire a steam locomotive, the thermal energy of a coal fire must be

   converted to the _____ energy of the moving train.

2. The conversion of thermal energy to mechanical energy requires a device

   called a(n) _____.

3. What is the process of burning a fuel, such as coal or gasoline?

   _____

4. How are heat engines classified? _____

   _____

   _____

5. Complete the compare/contrast table.

Heat Engines		
Type	**Where Fuel Is Burned**	**Example**
External combustion engines		
Internal combustion engines		

6. In a steam engine, what does the steam move back and forth inside a

   cylinder? _____

7. In an internal combustion engine, each up or down movement of a

   piston is called a(n) _____.

8. When a spark ignites the mixture of gas and fuel in a four-stroke engine,

   stored chemical energy is converted to _____ energy.

CHAPTER 6, Thermal Energy and Heat *(continued)*

9. Complete the flowchart below, which describes the process that occurs in each cylinder of a four-stroke engine.

A mixture of fuel and air is drawn into the cylinder during the _____ stroke.

↓

During the _____ stroke, the mixture is squeezed into a smaller space.

↓

A spark plug ignites the mixture during _____, heating up the gas.

↓

During the _____ stroke, the heated gas expands and pushes the piston down, which moves the crankshaft.

↓

During the _____ stroke, the piston pushes the heated gas out, making room for new fuel and air.

▶ Refrigerators (page 190)

10. A refrigerator transfers thermal energy from a cool area to a(n)

_____ area.

11. What provides the energy for a refrigerator to transfer energy from

inside to outside? _____

_____

12. Where does the gas that circulates through the tubes inside the

refrigerator walls lose thermal energy? _____

_____

Motion, Forces, and Energy

WordWise

Use the clues below to identify key terms from Chapter 6. Write the terms on the lines, putting one letter in each blank. When you finish, the word enclosed in the diagonal will reveal an important term related to kinetic energy.

Clues

1. The expanding of matter when it is heated
2. Thermal energy that is transferred
3. Process of burning a fuel
4. Process by which matter changes from the liquid to the gas state
5. Heat is transferred by the movement of these currents.
6. Vaporization that takes place at the surface of a liquid
7. A material that does not conduct heat well
8. The change of state from solid to liquid
9. The temperature at which no more energy can be removed from matter
10. A material that conducts heat well
11. The physical change from one state of matter to another

1. _ _ _ _ _ _   _ _ _ _ _ _ _ _
2. _ _ _ _
3. _ _ _ _ _ _ _ _
4. _ _ _ _ _ _ _ _ _ _
5. _ _ _ _ _ _ _ _ _ _
6. _ _ _ _ _ _ _ _ _ _
7. _ _ _ _ _ _ _ _ _
8. _ _ _ _ _ _ _
9. _ _ _ _ _ _ _ _ _   _ _ _ _
10. _ _ _ _ _ _ _ _
11. _ _ _ _ _   _ _   _ _ _ _ _

CHAPTER 6, Thermal Energy and Heat (continued)

MathWise

For the problems below, show your calculations. If you need more space, use another sheet of paper. Write the answers for the problems on the lines below.

▶ Specific Heat (pages 176–177)

1. Heat absorbed = (2 kg)(450 J/(kg·K))(5 K) = _____

2. Heat absorbed = (7 kg)(664 J/(kg·K))(20 K) = _____

3. Aluminum has a specific heat of 903 J/(kg·K). How much heat is required to raise the temperature of 6 kilograms of aluminum 15 kelvins?

   Answer: _____

4. Sand has a specific heat of 670 J/(kg·K). How much heat is required to raise the temperature of 16 kilograms of sand 5 kelvins?

   Answer: _____

5. Water has a specific heat of 4,180 J/(kg·K). How much heat is required to raise the temperature of 3 kilograms of water 20 kelvins?

   Answer: _____